Somali and English Words for School Use

Erayo Soomaali iyo Ingririiisi ah oo Dugsiyadu Isticmaalaan

BARCODE ON BACK COVER

How to Use This Book

Somali and English Words for School Use
Erayo Soomaali iyo Ingririisi ah oo Dugsiyadu Isticmaalaan
Abdillahi Osman Jama
Translated by Abdillahi Osman Jama
Additional material compiled by Jill Rutter
Photograph by Hamish Wilson
Designed by Artloud
Printed by Typecast
Copyright Refugee Council, 1998

the refugee council

Funding for this leaflet was generously provided by European Commission Directorate-General V
Registered as the British Refugee Council under the Charities Act 1960 No 1014576
Registered Company No 2727514
Registered Address 3 Bondway London SW8 1SJ

This book is one of a series of five illustrated classroom word lists in languages spoken by refugee children. It is targeted at children who are newly arrived in the UK and are beginning to learn English. It can also be used with children who have little or no literacy in Somali, to help them develop reading and writing skills in those languages.

Somali words are listed at the top of the illustrations. There are differences in dialect in Somali. As far as possible the book uses words that are understood by all Somalis, otherwise two or more words are listed. Further information about the Somali language is given on page 23.

The classroom words can be used in different ways, such as:

◆ to label pictures and classroom objects;

◆ to match pictures to names by using correcting fluid, you can erase English words, Somali words or the pictures. Sets of cards can be made without names or illustrations, which can then be matched by the pupil;

◆ to make games such as pelmanism, word bingo and snap;

◆ to help pupils construct simple sentences;

◆ to take home to copy, read and learn words, as an early homework task. All children who are beginning to learn English should be given homework if their classmates receive it, even though it needs to be very simple. Parents and carers can be encouraged to help their children with such tasks;

◆ to help students develop literacy in Somali.

My School **Dugsigayga**

Classroom **Qolka waxbarashada**

Dining room **Qolka cuntada**

Library **Kaydka kutubta**

Office **Xafiis**

Cloakroom **Qolka dharka**

Playground **Gegada ciyaarta**

Teacher **Bare**

Book **Kitaab**

Bookcase **Xerada kitaabka**

Exercise book **Kitaabka layliska**

Blackboard **Sabuurad**

Computer **Kombyuutar**

4

Toys **Qalabka qooqa**

Ball **Kubad**

Pen **Qalin rinji**

Pencil **Qalin bisil**

Scissors **Maqas**

Ruler **Mastarad**

Rubber **Masaxaad**

School bag **Shandada dugsiga**

Paintbrush **Bulayga rinjiga**

Chair **Kursi**

Table **Miis**

Clock **Saacad**

People **Dad**

Man **Nin**

Woman **Naag**

Children **Caruur**

Boy **Wiil**

Girl **Inan, Gabadh**

Baby **Ilma yar**

Doctor **Dhakhtar**

Nurse **Kaaliye caafimaad**

Farmer **Beerwale**

Secretary **Xog-haye**

Shop assistant **Kaaliye dukaan**

Carpenter **Nijaar**

Parts of the Body **Xubnaha**

Leg **Lug**

Foot **Cag**

Toe **Suul**

Arm **Gacan**

Hand **Gacan**

Finger **Far**

Head **Madax**

Hair **Timo**

Eye **Il**

Nose **San**

Mouth **Af**

Ear **Dheg**

Clothes **Maryo**

Shoes **Kabo**

Trainers **Kabo laylis**

Sandals **Sandhal**

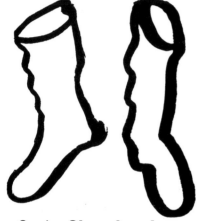

Socks **Sharabaado**

Coat **Koodh**

Hat **Koofiyad**

Trousers **Sirwaal dheer**

Shirt **Shaadh**

Jumper, Pullover **Funaanad lays-ka-siibo**

Skirt **Googarad**

Dress **Toob**

Tie **Taay**

8

Knickers, Pants
Surwaal hooseed hableed, Nigis Hableed

Vest **Gran gacmo go'an**

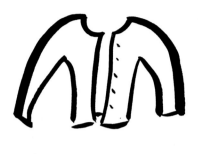

Cardigan **Funaanad laab furan**

Shorts **Sirwaal gaaban**

Tee-shirt **Garan gacmo gaaban**

Tights **Taaytis**

Watch **Sacad gacmeed**

Gloves **Fara gashi**

Raincoat **Kood roobeed**

Scarf **Masar**

Bag **Shandad**

Umbrella **Dalaayad**

9

Animals **Xayawaan**

Cow **Sac**

Calf **Weyl**

Sheep **Ido**

Lamb **Baraar**

Goat **Ri**

Pig **Doofaar**

Cat **Bisad**

Kitten **Bisad dhal ah**

Dog **Ey**

Puppy **Ey dhal ah**

Mouse **Walo**

Rabbit **Bakayle**

Fox **Dacawo**

Bird **Shimbir**

Elephant **Maroodi**

Lion **Libaax**

Monkey **Daayeer**

Bear **Dub**

Fly **Duqsi**

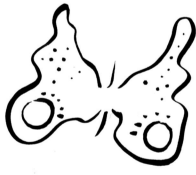

Butterfly **Balanbaalis**

Snake **Mas**

Worm **Dirxi**

Frog **Rah**

Bee **Shini**

Transport **Gaadiid**

Camel **Awr, Hal, Tulud**

Horse **Faras**

Tractor **Cagaf**

Lorry **Gaadhi xamuul**

Boat **Dooni**

Bicycle **Baskeelad**

Train **Tareen**

Bus **Bas**

Car **Gaadhi yar, Fatoorad**

Donkey **Dameer**

Pushchair **Kursiga ilmaha lagu riixo**

Aeroplane **Dayuurad**

Fruit and Vegetables **Qudrad**

Potato **Baradho**

Onion **Basal**

Tomato **Tamaandho, Yaanyo**

Carrot **Dabacase**

Cauliflower **Ubax kooli**

Lettuce **Saladh**

Cucumber **Khiyaar, Qanjaar**

Spinach **Isbinaaj**

Orange **Liin macaan**

Apple **Tufaax**

Banana **Muus**

Lemon **Liin dhanaan**

13

Food **Cunto**

Bread **Roodhi**

Fish **Kaluun**

Eggs **Beed, Ukun**

Chicken **Digaag, Dooro**

Meat **Hilib, Cad**

Cheese **Faar**

Sugar **Sonkor**

Flour **Daqiiq**

Rice **Bariis**

Salt **Milix**

Soup **Maraq**

Spagetti **Baasto**

Salad **Saladh**

Chips **Jibis,
Baradho shiilan**

Tea **Shaah**

Coffee **Bun, Qaxwe**

Milk **Caano**

Water **Biyo**

Biscuits **Buskud**

Cake **Keeg**

Sandwich **Saanwij**

Sweets **Nacnac**

Lentils **Lentils**

Tinned food **Cunto qasaac**

15

The Kitchen **Madbakha**

Cooker **Shoolad, Girgire**

Fridge **Talaagad**

Washing Machine **Qasaalad**

Sink **Berkad**

Cupboard **Kabadh**

Pans **Dheryo, Dusuud**

Knife **Middi**

Fork **Farageeto, Foog**

Spoon **Fandhaal, Qaado**

Plate **Saxan**

Cup **Koob**

Glass **Galaas**

The Bathroom Musqusha

Toilet **Baytalmay, Suuli**

Bath **Berkedda maydhashada**

Shower **Qubays**

Washbasin **Saxanka fool dhaqa**

Toothbrush **Caday**

Toothpaste **Dawo caday**

Teeth **Iiko**

Towel **Tuwaal**

Comb **Gadh feedh, Shanlo**

Soap **Saabuun**

Shampoo **Shaamboo**

Tap **Qasabad**

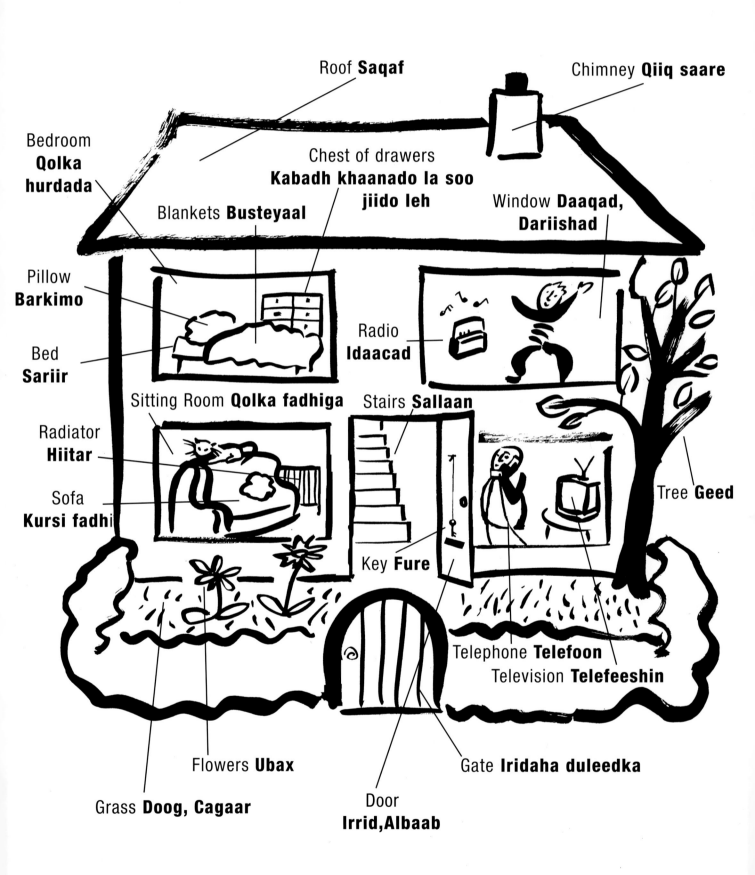

Roof **Saqaf**

Chimney **Qiiq saare**

Bedroom **Qolka hurdada**

Chest of drawers **Kabadh khaanado la soo jiido leh**

Window **Daaqad, Dariishad**

Blankets **Busteyaal**

Pillow **Barkimo**

Radio **Idaacad**

Bed **Sariir**

Sitting Room **Qolka fadhiga**

Stairs **Sallaan**

Radiator **Hiitar**

Tree **Geed**

Sofa **Kursi fadhi**

Key **Fure**

Telephone **Telefoon**

Television **Telefeeshin**

Flowers **Ubax**

Gate **Iridaha duleedka**

Grass **Doog, Cagaar**

Door **Irrid, Albaab**

My Street **Jidkayga**

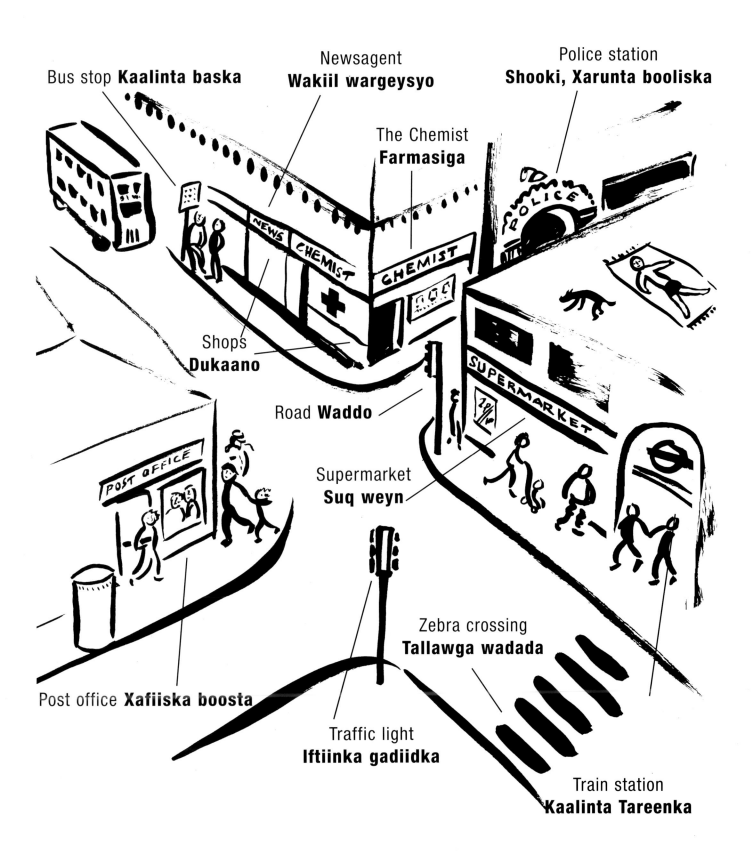

Bus stop **Kaalinta baska**

Newsagent **Wakiil wargeysyo**

Police station **Shooki, Xarunta booliska**

The Chemist **Farmasiga**

Shops **Dukaano**

Road **Waddo**

Supermarket **Suq weyn**

Post office **Xafiiska boosta**

Zebra crossing **Tallawga wadada**

Traffic light **Iftiinka gadiidka**

Train station **Kaalinta Tareenka**

Zero, Nought **Ibir**

One **Kow**

Two **Laba**

Three **Saddex**

Four **Afar**

Five **Shan**

Six **Lix**

Seven **Toddobo**

Eight **Siddeed**

Nine **Sagaal**

Ten **Toban**

One Hundred **Boqol**

Words and Phrases Erayo iyo Odhaaho

Yes **Haa**

No **Maya**

Please **Fadlan**

Thankyou **Mahadsanid**

Hello **Halaw**

Goodbye **Nabadgelyo**

My name is.... **Magacaygu waa ....**

My address is .... **Cinwaankaygu waa....**

My telephone number is ... **Telefoonkaygu waa ...**

My teacher's name is .... **Barahayga mag aciisu ...., Eedu waa....**

Cold **Qabow**

Hot **Kuleel**

I feel ill **Waxaan dareemayaa xanuun**

I have stomach **Che Waxa i haya calool xanuun**

I have a cold **Waxaan qabaa duray**

I have a headache **Waxa i haya madax xanuun**

Lessons Casharro

Maths **Xisaab**

English **Ingriisi**

Science **Saynis**

History **Taarikh**

Geography **Joqoraafi**

French **Faransiis**

Art **Fanka**

Music **Muusiqada**

PE/Games **Layliska jidhka, Ciyaaraha**

Meals Cunto

Breakfast **Afuro, Quraac**

Lunch **Hadhimo**

Supper/Dinner **Casho**

Left **Bidix**

Right **Midig**

Morning **Aroor**

Noon **Duhur**

Afternoon **Galab**

Evening **Fiid**

Night **Habeen**

Days of the week Maalmaha toddobaadka

Monday **Isniin**

Tuesday **Salaasa**

Wednesday **Arbaca**

Thursday **Khamiis**

Friday **Jimce**

Saturday **Sabti**

Sunday **Axad**

Months Bilaha

January **Janaayo**

February **Fabraayo**

March **Maarj**

April **Abril**

May **Meey**

June **Juun**

July **Julaay**

August **Ogos**

September **Sabtambar**

October **Oktoobar**

November **Noofambar**

December **Diisambar**

Seasons Xilliyada

Spring **Dayr**

Summer **Xagaa**

Autumn **Gu**

Winter **Jiilaal**

Weather Cimilada

Rain **Roob**

Sun **Qorax**

Wind **Dabayl**

Snow **Baraf**

Relatives Ehelka

Parents **Waalidiin**

Foster parents **Kafaala qaade caruur**

Father **Aabo**

Mother **Hooyo**

Son **Wiil**

Daughter **Gabadh**

Grandfather **Awow**

Grandmother **Ayeeyo**

Uncle (father's side) **Adeer**

Uncle (mother's side) **Abti**

Aunt (father's side) **Eddo**

Aunt (mother's side) **Habaryar**

Cousin **Ina-adeer**

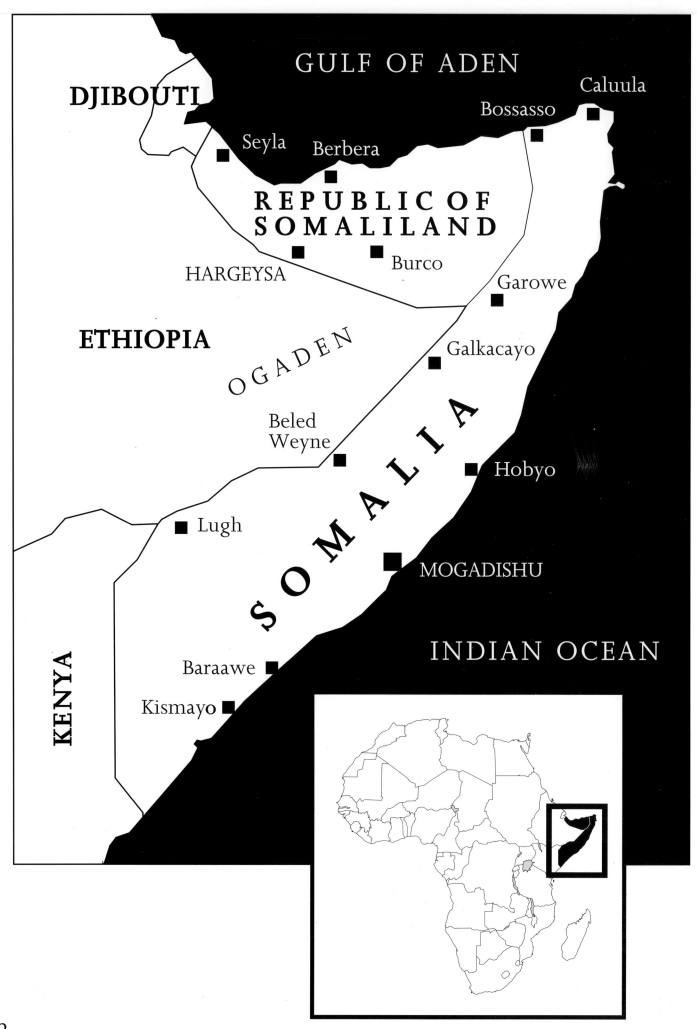

The Somali Language

Somali is the national language of Somalia and the unrecognised Republic of Somaliland. It is also spoken by over 1,500,000 people in the Ogaden region of Ethiopia, 300,000 people in Kenya and 125,000 people in Djibouti. Somali belongs to the Cushitic group of languages which is part of the Hamito-Semitic language family. Somali is most closely related to the languages spoken in the Ethiopian and Eritrean lowlands such as Oromo, Afar, Saho, Beja and Sidamo. Somali also uses words borrowed from Arabic or of Arabic origin.

The Somali language has several dialects. Somalis also speak in regional accents. The dialects are not always mutually intelligible, although most Somalis understand the northern dialects, which forms the basis for standard Somali. This book uses standard spoken Somali as far these words will be understood by the majority of children. Otherwise two or more words are listed. Written Somali also shows considerable differences in spelling as a standard spelling has not yet fully emerged. Spelling and word form are the subject of lively debate.

Somali is a phonetic language which uses the Roman alphabet. There are 21 consonants, five short vowels, five long vowels and five dipthongs. Although Somali is scripted in the Roman alphabet, the letters follow an Arabic-based ordering. Somali children will have to learn the ordering of letters when starting English.

Somali has a rich oral tradition of poems, proverbs and stories. Despite this, Somali remained an unscripted language until the late 1960s. In 1972 President Siad Barre decreed that the Roman alphabet would be used, and that Somali would become the sole official language of government and schooling. Urban literacy schemes were organised, and these were followed in 1974 by a rural literacy campaign. Over 25,000 students and older school children travelled to the rural areas to teach the new alphabet. High literacy rates were achieved. Educational achievement, however, is an early casualty of armed conflict. Schools have been destroyed by fighting in Somalia, and teachers have fled. As a result, many Somali refugee children arriving in Britain have had an interrupted or non-existent education. A significant number of children have limited literacy in Somali. In addition in the UK Somali refugee parents from rural areas or from poorer families may not be literate.

Many Somalis speak and read good Arabic. There are strong cultural links with Yemen. *Madrassah* (Koranic schools) worked alongside government schools in Somalia. In rural areas the *Madrassah* may be the only accessible school. Children attended *Madrassah* from an early age, learning Arabic. In the chaos of armed conflict in Mogadishu and other cities, it has been the *Madrassah* that have kept going. Some Somalis may have worked in the Gulf States and will speak Arabic as a result.

The exodus of refugees from Somalia has also included some minority groups. The Bravanese inhabit the town of Baraawe and other southern coastal towns. They speak Chimini (also known as Bravanese) as a first language. Chimini is a dialect of Swahili. Bravanese refugees have settled in east London and Manchester. Benadiris are an urban group who live in Mogadishu and other southern towns. The Reer Hamar are another urban minority group. Members of both groups may have Yemeni ancestry, and speak Arabic.

The Somali Alphabet

B as in bottle

T as in table

J as in jam

X pronounced as 'h' - the Somali name Xasan is pronounced as Hassan

KH is an uvular fricative 'kh', difficult for the native English speaker to pronounce.

D as in door

R as in rich

S as in salt

SH as in shop

DH pronounced as 'd'.

C pronounced as 'a' - the Somali name Cabdi is pronounced as Abdi

G as in garden

F as in father

Q pronounced as 'ka' - Qatar

K as in cat

L as in lamb

M as in mouse

N as in not

W as in week

H as in hat

Y as in yellow

Short Vowels

A as in hat

E as in elf

I as in hit

O as in hot

U as in book

Long Vowels

AA as in far

EE as in air

II as in seed

OO as in door

UU as in food

Dipthongs

AY as in tie

AW as in cow

EY as in may

OY as in boy

OW as in boat